Through the Lens: Capturing the Beauty of Nature and Wildlife

Welcome to "Through the Lens: Capturing the Beauty of Nature and Wildlife." In this book, we embark on a visual journey into the enchanting world of nature and wildlife photography. Through the lens of talented photographers, we will explore the awe-inspiring landscapes, fascinating creatures, and breathtaking moments found in the natural world.

Nature and wildlife photography is a captivating art form that allows us to witness the splendor of our planet and the diverse life it harbors. It offers a glimpse into the intricate ecosystems and the delicate balance between species and their environments. It is through the lens that we can truly appreciate the beauty, intricacy, and vulnerability of the natural world.

In "Through the Lens," we will delve into the techniques, skills, and perspectives that make nature and wildlife photography a unique and rewarding pursuit. We will learn about the equipment and gear necessary to capture stunning images, as well as the technical aspects of composition, lighting, and exposure that bring photographs to life.

But this book is more than just a technical guide. It is a celebration of nature's wonders and a call to protect and preserve our fragile ecosystems. Through the captivating images and narratives within these pages, we aim to inspire a deeper connection to nature and a greater appreciation for its conservation.

Whether you are an aspiring photographer, a nature enthusiast, or simply someone who appreciates the beauty of the natural world, "Through the Lens" invites you to embark on a visual adventure and discover the extraordinary stories waiting to be told through nature and wildlife photography.

Join us as we delve into the captivating world of nature and wildlife photography and uncover the secrets, challenges, and rewards that await those who dare to capture the beauty of our planet "Through the Lens."

1. Introduction
   - Welcome to the world of nature and wildlife photography
   - The purpose and scope of the book
2. The Art of Nature and Wildlife Photography
   - Understanding the essence of nature and wildlife photography
   - Exploring the unique challenges and rewards of the genre
   - The role of storytelling and capturing moments in nature
3. Equipment and Gear
   - Essential cameras, lenses, and accessories for nature photography
   - Understanding the technical aspects of equipment selection
   - Tips for choosing the right gear for different environments and subjects
4. Mastering Composition and Lighting
   - Principles of composition for impactful nature and wildlife photographs
   - Utilizing natural light to enhance your images
   - Creative techniques for capturing dynamic and

visually striking shots
5. Field Techniques and Ethics
   - Approaching wildlife respectfully and responsibly
   - Strategies for finding and observing wildlife in their natural habitats
   - Tips for capturing unique perspectives and intimate moments
6. Post-Processing and Image Enhancement
   - Introduction to post-processing software and tools
   - Techniques for enhancing and optimizing nature and wildlife photographs
   - Preserving the authenticity of the image while enhancing its visual impact
7. Specialized Techniques and Subjects
   - Macro photography: Exploring the intricate details of nature up close
   - Bird and wildlife photography: Techniques for capturing fast-moving subjects
   - Landscape photography: Creating breathtaking vistas and capturing natural wonders
8. Conservation and Ethics in Nature Photography
   - The role of nature photographers as advocates for conservation
   - Promoting ethical practices and minimizing the impact on wildlife and habitats
   - The power of photography in raising awareness and inspiring action
9. Showcasing Your Work
   - Building a portfolio of nature and wildlife photographs
   - Opportunities for exhibiting and publishing your work
   - Sharing your passion for nature photography through digital platforms and social media

10. Inspiring Stories from Nature Photographers
  - Interviews and profiles of renowned nature and wildlife photographers
  - Their experiences, challenges, and insights into capturing the beauty of nature
  - Learning from their techniques and perspectives

11. Conclusion
  - Reflecting on the impact of nature and wildlife photography
  - Encouragement to continue exploring and appreciating the beauty of the natural world "Through the Lens"

Welcome to the world of nature and wildlife photography

Welcome to the world of nature and wildlife photography! In "Through the Lens: Capturing the Beauty of Nature and Wildlife," we embark on an exciting journey that celebrates the wonders of the natural world and the art of capturing its breathtaking moments.

Nature and wildlife photography is a passion-driven pursuit that allows us to immerse ourselves in the awe-inspiring beauty and diversity of the earth's ecosystems. It is a medium through which we can share our love for nature, raise awareness about environmental issues, and inspire others to appreciate and protect our natural heritage.

This book is a comprehensive guide that takes you through the intricacies of nature and wildlife photography, offering insights, tips, and techniques to help you elevate your skills and create stunning images. Whether you are a beginner eager to explore this captivating genre or an experienced photographer looking to refine your craft, this book is designed to inspire and empower you on your photographic journey.

Throughout the pages of "Through the Lens," we delve into various aspects of nature and wildlife photography. From understanding the essence of the genre and the unique challenges it presents to mastering the technical aspects of equipment selection and capturing compelling moments, we leave no stone unturned in our quest to help you tell compelling visual stories through your lens.

Beyond the technical aspects, we also delve into the artistic and creative elements of nature and wildlife photography. We explore the importance of composition, light, and timing in creating impactful images, and we discuss the ethical considerations involved in photographing wildlife and preserving the natural environment.

Furthermore, we showcase the work of renowned nature and wildlife photographers who have dedicated their lives to capturing the beauty of the natural world. Their inspiring stories and stunning imagery will ignite your passion and provide you with a glimpse into the possibilities that await as you embark on your own photographic adventures.

"Through the Lens: Capturing the Beauty of Nature and Wildlife" is an invitation to immerse yourself in the wonders of nature, to explore its untamed landscapes, and to embrace the challenges and rewards of photographing its inhabitants. It is a celebration of the artistry and craft behind nature and wildlife photography and a tribute to the power of imagery to inspire, educate, and foster a deep connection with the natural world.

Join us as we embark on this extraordinary journey, where every page is an invitation to witness and preserve the beauty of nature through the lens of your camera. Let's explore, learn, and capture the remarkable moments that unfold in the world around us, and in doing so, let's become advocates for the preservation and appreciation of our planet's precious ecosystems.

Welcome to "Through the Lens: Capturing the Beauty of Nature and Wildlife." Let the adventure begin!

The purpose and scope of the book

The purpose of "Through the Lens: Capturing the Beauty of Nature and Wildlife" is to serve as a comprehensive guide for nature and wildlife photography enthusiasts, offering valuable insights, practical tips, and artistic inspiration. The book aims to inspire and empower readers to explore the wonders of the natural world, develop their technical skills, and unleash their creativity through the lens of their camera.

The scope of the book encompasses various aspects of nature and wildlife photography, including equipment selection, technical considerations, composition, lighting, storytelling, ethical practices, and post-processing techniques. It covers a wide range of topics, from understanding the essence of the genre to mastering the art of capturing compelling moments in nature.

In addition to the technical aspects, the book also explores the emotional and artistic elements of nature and wildlife photography. It delves into the connection between the photographer and the natural world, encouraging readers to develop a deeper appreciation for nature and to capture its beauty in a way that evokes emotion and tells a visual story.

Furthermore, "Through the Lens" showcases the work of renowned nature and wildlife photographers, providing a source of inspiration and motivation for readers. It highlights their unique perspectives, techniques, and approaches to photographing the natural world, offering valuable insights into the creative process and the possibilities that await those who embark on this captivating photographic journey.

Overall, the book aims to be a comprehensive resource for

both beginner and experienced photographers, offering practical guidance, artistic inspiration, and a deeper understanding of the art and craft of nature and wildlife photography. It encourages readers to explore and appreciate the beauty of the natural world, while also advocating for its preservation and conservation.

Understanding the essence of nature and wildlife photography

Understanding the essence of nature and wildlife photography is crucial for capturing the beauty and significance of the natural world. It goes beyond simply taking pictures of animals or landscapes; it involves connecting with nature on a deeper level and conveying its essence through visual storytelling.

Nature photography is about capturing the awe-inspiring landscapes, the intricate details of flora and fauna, and the remarkable moments of animal behavior. It allows us to witness and appreciate the diversity and wonders of the natural world, while wildlife photography focuses specifically on capturing animals in their natural habitats, showcasing their behavior, beauty, and sometimes their vulnerability.

To truly understand the essence of nature and wildlife photography, one must cultivate a deep respect and love for nature. It requires patience, observation, and an understanding of animal behavior and habitats. It involves immersing oneself in the environment, observing the play of light, anticipating moments of action or stillness, and capturing the unique interactions between animals and their surroundings.

Nature and wildlife photography also have a strong conservation component. Through the lens, photographers have the opportunity to raise awareness about the fragility of ecosystems, the importance of biodiversity, and the need for environmental stewardship. By capturing the beauty and vulnerability of nature, photographers can inspire others to appreciate and protect the natural world.

In essence, nature and wildlife photography is a powerful medium for storytelling, evoking emotions, and fostering a connection between viewers and the natural world. It allows us to celebrate the beauty of our planet, highlight its delicate balance, and advocate for its preservation. It is an art form that requires technical skill, artistic vision, and a deep appreciation for the natural world.

Exploring the unique challenges and rewards of the genre

Exploring the world of nature and wildlife photography comes with its own set of unique challenges and rewards. While the rewards are plentiful, it is important to acknowledge and understand the challenges that photographers face in this genre.

One of the primary challenges of nature and wildlife photography is the unpredictability of the subjects. Animals can be elusive, shy, and quick to retreat into their natural habitats, making it challenging to capture the perfect shot. Patience, persistence, and a deep understanding of animal behavior are essential to overcome these challenges.

Another challenge is working with natural lighting conditions. The dynamic nature of outdoor environments means that photographers must adapt to changing light throughout the day, dealing with harsh sunlight, low light situations, and unpredictable weather conditions. The ability to make the most of available light and utilize techniques such as exposure compensation and proper white balance is crucial.

Additionally, nature and wildlife photographers often find themselves in remote and physically demanding locations. They may need to trek through rugged terrains, endure extreme temperatures, or spend long hours waiting in uncomfortable conditions. The dedication to capturing that extraordinary moment often requires sacrifices and a love for adventure and exploration.

However, the rewards of nature and wildlife photography are unparalleled. It offers the opportunity to witness the breathtaking beauty of landscapes and the intimate moments of animal behavior that most people rarely get to experience. The sense of accomplishment that comes with capturing a unique and compelling image is incredibly rewarding.

Nature and wildlife photography also provides a deeper connection to the natural world. It allows photographers to appreciate the intricate details of nature, learn about different ecosystems, and gain a profound understanding of the importance of conservation. Through their images, photographers have the power to inspire others, raise awareness about environmental issues, and contribute to the protection of our planet's biodiversity.

In conclusion, the challenges of nature and wildlife photography are surpassed by the immense rewards it offers. It is a genre that requires dedication, technical skill, and a deep passion for nature. The ability to capture the beauty and diversity of the natural world and share it with others is both a privilege and a responsibility for nature and wildlife photographers.

The role of storytelling and capturing moments in nature

In nature and wildlife photography, storytelling and capturing moments play a vital role in creating powerful and impactful images. While technical skills and equipment are important, it is the ability to tell a story and evoke emotions through photographs that sets nature and wildlife photography apart.

Through careful observation and anticipation, photographers aim to capture decisive moments that convey a narrative or evoke a specific feeling. They seek to capture the essence of a particular scene or behavior, whether it's the tenderness of a mother caring for her offspring, the intensity of a predator in pursuit, or the serene beauty of a landscape at sunrise. These moments have the power to transport viewers to the natural world, evoking a sense of wonder and connection.

Storytelling in nature photography goes beyond individual images. It involves creating a series of photographs that collectively tell a larger narrative. Photographers may document the life cycle of a particular species, the changing seasons in a specific location, or the impact of human activities on the environment. By presenting a cohesive story, photographers can educate, raise awareness, and inspire action towards conservation and preservation.

To capture these moments and tell a compelling story, photographers must develop a deep understanding and knowledge of their subjects. They immerse themselves in the natural environment, learning about animal behavior, habitats, and ecosystems. This allows them to anticipate and be in the right place at the right time to capture those fleeting moments that tell a story.

Furthermore, composition, light, and technical choices also contribute to the storytelling aspect of nature and wildlife photography. Photographers carefully consider the framing, perspective, and visual elements within the frame to guide the viewer's eye and convey the intended narrative. The use of light, whether it's the warm golden light of sunset or the dramatic contrast of shadows, adds depth and emotion to the image, enhancing the storytelling aspect.

In summary, storytelling and capturing moments are essential elements of nature and wildlife photography. Through skilled observation, anticipation, and technical proficiency, photographers can create images that go beyond mere documentation. They tell stories that inspire, inform, and ignite a passion for the natural world, fostering a deeper appreciation for its beauty and the need for its protection.

Essential cameras, lenses, and accessories for nature photography

Nature photography requires specialized equipment to capture the beauty and intricacies of the natural world. Here are some essential cameras, lenses, and accessories commonly used by nature photographers:

1. Camera: A digital single-lens reflex (DSLR) or mirrorless camera with manual control capabilities is preferred for its versatility and image quality. Look for a camera with a high-resolution sensor, good low-light performance, and weather sealing to withstand outdoor conditions.

2. Telephoto Lens: A telephoto lens is essential for capturing wildlife and distant subjects. A lens with a focal length of 200mm or longer is recommended, such as a 300mm, 400mm, or 600mm lens. This allows you to zoom in on wildlife and capture detailed images from a distance.

3. Wide-Angle Lens: A wide-angle lens is useful for capturing expansive landscapes, environmental portraits, and dramatic perspectives. A lens with a focal length of around 24mm to 35mm is commonly used for nature photography.

4. Macro Lens: A macro lens is ideal for photographing small subjects, such as insects, flowers, and textures in nature. Look for a lens with a 1:1 magnification ratio to capture intricate details.

5. Tripod: A sturdy tripod is essential for achieving sharp images, especially in low-light situations and for

long-exposure photography. Look for a tripod that is lightweight, durable, and easily adjustable.

6. Filters: Filters can enhance your nature photography by controlling light and reducing glare. Consider using a polarizing filter to reduce reflections and enhance colors, a neutral density (ND) filter to control exposure in bright conditions, and a graduated ND filter for balancing exposure in landscapes with bright skies.

7. Camera Bag: A reliable and comfortable camera bag is essential for protecting and carrying your gear while out in nature. Look for a bag that is durable, weather-resistant, and has compartments for organizing your equipment.

8. Remote Shutter Release: A remote shutter release or cable release allows you to trigger the camera without touching it, reducing the risk of camera shake and ensuring sharp images, especially for long-exposure photography and wildlife photography.

9. Extra Batteries and Memory Cards: Nature photography often involves spending extended periods in the field. It is crucial to have extra camera batteries and memory cards to avoid running out of power or storage space.

10. Cleaning Kit: Keep a cleaning kit handy to remove dust, dirt, and smudges from your lenses and camera body. A microfiber cloth, blower brush, and lens cleaning solution are commonly used for cleaning and maintenance.

Remember, the specific equipment you choose will depend on your photography style, budget, and the type of nature subjects you wish to capture. It's important to research and invest in quality gear that suits your needs and allows you to express your creative vision in the world of nature photography.

Understanding the technical aspects of equipment selection

When it comes to selecting photography equipment for nature and wildlife photography, there are several technical aspects to consider. These include:

1. Sensor Size: The sensor size of a camera affects image quality and low-light performance. Larger sensors generally produce better image quality and have better noise performance in low-light conditions.

2. Megapixels: The number of megapixels determines the resolution of the image. Higher megapixel count allows for greater detail and the ability to crop images while maintaining good quality.

3. ISO Performance: ISO sensitivity refers to the camera's ability to capture images in low-light situations. Look for a camera with good high ISO performance to ensure clean and noise-free images when shooting in challenging lighting conditions.

4. Autofocus System: Nature and wildlife photography often involve fast-moving subjects. A camera with a reliable and fast autofocus system with advanced tracking capabilities can help you capture sharp images of animals in action.

5. Frames per Second (FPS): The frames per second or burst rate indicates how many photos a camera can capture in rapid succession. A higher FPS is beneficial for capturing fast action and ensuring you don't miss crucial moments.

6. Weather Sealing: Since nature photography often takes place in outdoor environments, it's essential to choose a camera and lenses with weather sealing to protect against dust, moisture, and extreme temperatures.

7. Lens Compatibility: Consider the availability of lenses for your chosen camera system. Nature photography often requires specialized lenses, such as telephoto and macro lenses, to capture distant wildlife or intricate details. Ensure the camera system you choose offers a range of lens options.

8. Image Stabilization: Optical or sensor-based image stabilization can help compensate for camera shake, allowing you to shoot handheld at slower shutter speeds without compromising image sharpness.

9. Battery Life: Nature photography can be time-consuming and may require extended periods in the field. A camera with long battery life is crucial to ensure you don't run out of power during your photo outings.

10. Ergonomics and Size: Consider the ergonomics and size of the camera, as well as the weight of lenses and accessories. Nature photography often involves carrying equipment for long durations, so it's important to choose gear that is comfortable and manageable for your needs.

It's important to balance your budget and specific requirements when selecting equipment. Prioritize the features that are most important to your style of nature photography and invest in lenses and accessories that complement your chosen camera system. Remember, the right equipment should empower you to capture stunning images of nature and wildlife and bring your creative vision to life.

Tips for choosing the right gear for different environments and subjects

When choosing gear for different environments and subjects in nature and wildlife photography, consider the following tips:

1. Research and Plan: Understand the specific requirements of your intended environment and subjects. Different environments, such as forests, deserts, or underwater, may require specialized equipment. Similarly, certain subjects like birds, mammals, or macro subjects have specific gear considerations.

2. Evaluate Your Needs: Assess your shooting style, preferences, and budget. Determine the focal length range you'll need, such as wide-angle for landscapes or telephoto for wildlife. Consider the level of portability and convenience you require for your shooting expeditions.

3. Lenses: Invest in high-quality lenses suited for your intended subjects. Wide-angle lenses are ideal for landscapes, while telephoto lenses are essential for capturing distant wildlife. Macro lenses are useful for close-up shots of small subjects like insects and flowers. Consider factors like maximum aperture, image stabilization, and weather sealing.

4. Accessories: Depending on your shooting conditions, consider accessories like tripods, monopods, or gimbal heads for stability when using telephoto lenses. Filters, such as polarizers or neutral density filters, can enhance

the quality of your images and allow for creative effects. Additional accessories like remote shutter releases, flash units, and diffusers can also be helpful.

5. Camera Features: Look for cameras with advanced autofocus systems, fast burst rates, and excellent low-light performance. Consider features like built-in image stabilization, weather sealing, and customizable settings that suit your shooting style.

6. Portability and Durability: Evaluate the weight and size of your gear, especially if you plan to hike or travel long distances. Consider lighter options without compromising image quality. Also, choose gear with durability and weather resistance to withstand outdoor conditions.

7. Test and Rent Equipment: Before making a significant investment, try out different gear if possible. Renting equipment allows you to assess its performance and suitability for your needs before committing to a purchase.

8. Stay Informed: Keep up with the latest advancements in camera technology and lens releases. Read reviews, consult photography forums, and seek advice from experienced photographers to make informed decisions.

Remember, the right gear should support your creative vision and enable you to capture stunning images in various environments and subjects. Consider your shooting preferences, adaptability, and the demands of each situation to choose the gear that best suits your needs.

Principles of composition for impactful nature and wildlife photographs

To create impactful nature and wildlife photographs, it's essential to apply principles of composition. Here are some key principles to keep in mind:

1. Rule of Thirds: Divide your frame into a grid of nine equal sections using two horizontal and two vertical lines. Position your main subject or points of interest along these lines or at their intersections to create a visually pleasing composition.

2. Leading Lines: Utilize natural elements like paths, rivers, branches, or tree lines to lead the viewer's eye into the frame and towards the main subject. Leading lines add depth and guide the viewer's gaze through the image.

3. Balance and Symmetry: Aim for a balanced distribution of visual weight in your composition. Symmetrical subjects or scenes can create a sense of harmony and stability, while asymmetrical compositions can add visual interest and tension. Experiment with both to create dynamic compositions.

4. Depth and Layering: Incorporate foreground, middle ground, and background elements to create a sense of depth in your photographs. This adds dimension and can make the viewer feel immersed in the scene.

5. Framing and Negative Space: Use natural elements like tree branches, arches, or rock formations to frame your subject and draw attention to it. Negative space, the empty areas around your subject, can emphasize its

importance and create a sense of simplicity and focus.

6. Point of View and Perspective: Explore different angles and perspectives to create unique and engaging compositions. Get down low, shoot from high above, or try unconventional angles to provide a fresh and captivating view of your subject.

7. Patterns and Textures: Look for patterns, repetition, and textures in nature to add visual interest to your photographs. They can create a sense of rhythm and add a tactile element to your images.

8. Lighting and Golden Hour: Pay attention to lighting conditions, as it can dramatically impact the mood and atmosphere of your photographs. Soft, warm light during the golden hour (shortly after sunrise or before sunset) can enhance the beauty of nature and wildlife subjects.

Remember, these principles serve as guidelines, but creativity and experimentation are also essential. Develop your own style and use these principles as a foundation to capture impactful and visually compelling nature and wildlife photographs.

Utilizing natural light to enhance your images

Utilizing natural light effectively is crucial for enhancing the quality and impact of your nature and wildlife images. Here are some tips to help you make the most of natural light:

1. Golden Hour: Take advantage of the golden hour, which occurs during the first hour after sunrise and the last hour before sunset. The soft, warm light during this time can add a beautiful, golden glow to your subjects and create a more pleasing atmosphere.

2. Soft Light: Seek out diffused or indirect light, which can be found on overcast days or in shaded areas. Soft light helps minimize harsh shadows and creates a more even and flattering illumination for your subjects.

3. Backlighting: Experiment with backlighting, where the light source is positioned behind your subject. This can create a halo effect, highlighting the edges of your subject and adding depth and drama to your images.

4. Side Lighting: When the sun is low in the sky, the angle of light creates interesting shadows and textures. Side lighting can accentuate details, such as the texture of fur or feathers, and create a sense of depth in your photographs.

5. Avoid Harsh Midday Sun: During midday when the sun is high in the sky, the light is harsh and can create strong shadows and overexposed areas. If possible, avoid shooting during this time or find shaded areas to minimize the harshness of the light.

6. Experiment with Shadows: Shadows can add depth and dimension to your images. Look for interesting

shadow patterns or play with shadows to create unique compositions and visual interest.

7. Reflectors and Diffusers: Use reflectors or diffusers to manipulate and control the natural light. Reflectors bounce light onto your subject, filling in shadows, while diffusers soften and diffuse harsh light.

8. Silhouettes and Sunbursts: Capture silhouettes against a bright background to create dramatic and artistic images. Sunbursts can be achieved by shooting into the sun using a narrow aperture (higher f-number), creating a star-like effect around the sun.

Remember, the quality and direction of natural light can vary depending on the time of day, weather conditions, and location. Take the time to observe and understand how light interacts with your subjects, and experiment with different lighting techniques to create stunning and captivating nature and wildlife photographs.

Creative techniques for capturing dynamic and visually striking shots

To capture dynamic and visually striking shots in nature and wildlife photography, here are some creative techniques you can try:

1. Motion Blur: Experiment with intentional motion blur to convey a sense of movement. You can achieve this by using a slow shutter speed and panning with a moving subject or capturing the movement of water, wind-blown leaves, or flying birds.

2. Freeze the Action: On the other hand, freezing the action can also create impactful images. Use a fast shutter speed to capture the precise moment of action, whether it's a bird in flight, a running animal, or a splashing water droplet.

3. Close-ups and Macro Photography: Get up close and personal with your subjects to reveal intricate details and textures. Macro photography allows you to explore the miniature world of insects, flowers, and other small subjects, revealing their beauty and complexity.

4. Unconventional Angles: Break away from traditional perspectives and experiment with unique angles and viewpoints. Get low to the ground for a worm's-eye view or climb higher for a bird's-eye view. These unconventional angles can add drama and a fresh perspective to your photographs.

5. Reflections: Seek out bodies of water or other reflective surfaces to capture reflections of your subjects.

Reflections can add a sense of symmetry, depth, and visual interest to your images.

6. Patterns and Textures: Look for patterns and textures in nature, such as the symmetry of a flower petal, the repetition of tree bark, or the scales of a reptile. These elements can create visually captivating and abstract compositions.

7. Framing: Use natural elements like tree branches, leaves, or rock formations to frame your subject and draw attention to it. Framing adds depth and context to your image, creating a more engaging composition.

8. Environmental Portraits: Capture your subject in its natural habitat, showcasing the relationship between the subject and its surroundings. This approach can provide a storytelling element and give viewers a glimpse into the subject's world.

9. Silhouettes: Play with silhouettes against a bright or colorful background. Silhouettes can create a striking contrast between the dark subject and the vibrant sky, sunset, or other elements in the frame.

10. Creative Use of Depth of Field: Experiment with shallow depth of field to isolate your subject from the background, creating a dreamy and ethereal effect. Alternatively, use a deep depth of field to keep the entire scene in focus, revealing the context and surroundings of your subject.

Remember, creativity in nature and wildlife photography comes from experimentation and pushing the boundaries. Don't be afraid to try new techniques, embrace the unexpected, and let your artistic vision guide you to capture dynamic and visually striking shots.

Approaching wildlife respectfully and responsibly

When photographing wildlife, it's essential to approach them with respect and prioritize their well-being. Here are some guidelines for approaching wildlife responsibly:

1. Keep a Safe Distance: Maintain a respectful distance from the animals to avoid causing stress or disturbance. Use telephoto lenses or zoom capabilities to get close-up shots without intruding on their space.

2. Observe from a Distance: Take the time to observe the animals' behavior and movements from afar before attempting to photograph them. This will help you understand their comfort level and determine if it's appropriate to approach closer.

3. Do Not Disturb or Alter Habitat: Avoid altering the natural environment or disturbing the animals' habitat. Refrain from removing vegetation or interfering with nests or dens. Leave no trace and minimize your impact on the surroundings.

4. Be Patient: Wildlife photography often requires patience. Allow the animals to acclimate to your presence and continue with their natural activities. Patience allows for more authentic and candid shots without disrupting their behavior.

5. Respect Protected Areas and Regulations: Familiarize yourself with the rules and regulations of the area you're photographing in, especially if it's a protected wildlife reserve or national park. Follow the guidelines set by

park authorities to ensure the safety of the wildlife and maintain the integrity of the ecosystem.

6. Avoid Feeding or Provoking Wildlife: Feeding wildlife can disrupt their natural foraging patterns and create dependency on humans. It can also pose risks to their health and safety. Avoid enticing or provoking animals for the sake of a photograph.

7. Use a Silent and Non-intrusive Approach: Minimize noise and sudden movements when approaching wildlife. Using a quiet camera with a silent shooting mode can help reduce any potential disturbance. Avoid flash photography unless necessary and permitted.

8. Educate Yourself: Learn about the behavior and habitat of the wildlife you're photographing. Understanding their natural tendencies will enable you to predict their movements and capture more meaningful images.

9. Support Conservation Efforts: Use your photography to raise awareness about wildlife conservation and support organizations dedicated to protecting and preserving natural habitats. Share your images responsibly, promoting appreciation and understanding of the animals and their environment.

Remember, the welfare of the animals should always come first. By approaching wildlife responsibly, you can capture compelling photographs while ensuring their well-being and the conservation of their habitats.

Strategies for finding and observing wildlife in their natural habitats

Finding and observing wildlife in their natural habitats can be a rewarding experience for nature photographers. Here are some strategies to help you locate and observe wildlife effectively:

1. Research and Plan: Before heading out, research the specific habitats, seasons, and behaviors of the wildlife you wish to photograph. Understanding their preferences and patterns will increase your chances of finding them.

2. Scout Potential Locations: Look for wildlife-rich areas such as national parks, wildlife reserves, wetlands, forests, or coastal areas. Seek recommendations from local guides, fellow photographers, or online forums to discover hidden gems.

3. Time of Day: Many animals are most active during early mornings and late afternoons, known as the "golden hours." Plan your outings during these times to maximize your chances of encountering wildlife.

4. Blend In: Wear neutral, earth-toned clothing that blends with the surroundings to avoid startling or alarming the animals. Avoid wearing bright colors that may attract unnecessary attention.

5. Move Slowly and Silently: Approach your chosen location or wildlife sighting area with care. Move slowly and quietly, minimizing sudden movements or loud noises that may startle or disturb the animals.

6. Be Patient: Wildlife encounters can be unpredictable.

VIKASH DABRIWAL

Settle into a comfortable position and be patient. Spend time observing and waiting for wildlife to appear or for interesting behaviors to unfold.

7. Use Binoculars or Telephoto Lenses: Binoculars or a telephoto lens will help you spot wildlife from a distance. Use them to scan the area, identify potential subjects, and assess their behavior before deciding to approach closer.

8. Look for Signs: Learn to identify signs of wildlife presence, such as tracks, droppings, feathers, or sounds. These indications can guide you toward potential sightings and increase your chances of finding wildlife.

9. Hire Local Guides: Consider engaging local guides who have in-depth knowledge of the area and its wildlife. Their expertise and familiarity with animal behaviors can greatly enhance your wildlife photography experience.

10. Practice Fieldcraft: Develop fieldcraft skills, such as camouflage techniques, scent control, and knowledge of wind direction, to get closer to wildlife without alarming them. These skills can help you blend into the environment and capture more intimate shots.

Remember to always prioritize the well-being of the animals and respect their natural habitats. Keep a safe distance and refrain from disturbing or interfering with their behavior. Wildlife photography should be done responsibly, with the utmost consideration for the welfare of the subjects and the preservation of their ecosystems.

Tips for capturing unique perspectives and intimate moments

Capturing unique perspectives and intimate moments in nature and wildlife photography can make your images stand out and evoke a deeper connection with the viewers. Here are some tips to help you achieve that:

1. Experiment with Angles: Get creative with your camera angles and perspectives. Instead of shooting at eye level, try shooting from a low angle or a high vantage point. Changing your perspective can provide a fresh and unique view of your subject.

2. Get Close and Fill the Frame: To capture intimate moments, try to get as close to your subject as possible. Use a telephoto lens or employ cropping techniques in post-processing to fill the frame with your subject, emphasizing the details and expressions.

3. Focus on Details: Sometimes, the smallest details can tell a compelling story. Zoom in on intricate patterns, textures, or body parts of your subject to create visually captivating images that reveal hidden beauty.

4. Patience and Observation: Spend time observing and anticipating the behavior of your subjects. Patience is key to capturing those intimate moments when animals display interesting behaviors or interactions. Stay alert and ready to capture the decisive moment.

5. Use Depth of Field Creatively: Experiment with shallow depth of field to isolate your subject from the background, creating a sense of intimacy and focus.

Alternatively, use a wide depth of field to capture the environment and context surrounding your subject.

6. Seek Eye Contact: The eyes of your subject can be a powerful focal point in a photograph. Aim to capture eye contact, as it can create a connection between the viewer and the subject, conveying emotion and intimacy.

7. Wait for Golden Light: Take advantage of the warm, soft light during the golden hours (early morning and late afternoon). This light enhances the mood of your images and can add a sense of intimacy and magic to the scene.

8. Embrace Candid Moments: Some of the most authentic and intimate moments occur when animals are unaware of the camera. Be patient and observant, ready to capture candid moments that showcase the natural behavior and expressions of your subjects.

9. Use Negative Space: Experiment with negative space to create a sense of solitude or emphasize the smallness of your subject in the vastness of its environment. This technique can evoke a feeling of intimacy and serenity in your images.

10. Tell a Story: Look for opportunities to capture a series of images that tell a story or convey a narrative. Show the progression of events, interactions between subjects, or the context of the environment to engage the viewers and create a sense of intimacy.

Remember, building a connection with your subject and creating intimate moments in your photographs requires patience, observation, and a deep appreciation for the natural world. Respect the wildlife, maintain ethical practices, and prioritize their well-being throughout your photography journey.

Introduction to post-processing software and tools

Post-processing plays a crucial role in enhancing and refining your nature and wildlife photographs. It allows you to bring out the full potential of your images, fine-tune colors and tones, and add creative effects. In this section, we will explore the world of post-processing software and tools that can help you take your images to the next level.

1. Introduction to Editing Software: Get acquainted with popular post-processing software such as Adobe Lightroom, Adobe Photoshop, Capture One, and DxO PhotoLab. These software offer a wide range of powerful tools and features for adjusting exposure, color balance, contrast, and more.

2. Raw Image Processing: Learn the benefits of shooting in raw format and the capabilities it provides in post-processing. Raw files contain more data and allow for greater flexibility in adjusting exposure, recovering highlights and shadows, and fine-tuning white balance.

3. Basic Adjustments: Explore the essential adjustments you can make to enhance your images, such as adjusting exposure, contrast, highlights, shadows, and white balance. Learn how to use tools like sliders, curves, and levels to achieve the desired look.

4. Color Correction and Enhancement: Understand how to fine-tune colors and tones to create a harmonious and visually appealing image. Adjust color saturation, vibrance, and hue, as well as individual color channels.

Use tools like color grading and split toning to add a creative touch.

5. Sharpening and Noise Reduction: Discover techniques to enhance image sharpness and reduce noise in your photographs. Learn how to apply selective sharpening and noise reduction to maintain image quality while minimizing unwanted artifacts.

6. Creative Effects and Filters: Dive into the realm of creative possibilities by exploring various effects and filters. Experiment with vignetting, graduated filters, and radial filters to draw attention to your subject or create a specific mood. Explore black and white conversion techniques to add drama and impact.

7. Local Adjustments: Understand the power of local adjustments to selectively enhance specific areas of your image. Use tools like adjustment brushes, gradient filters, and spot healing to target and modify specific regions, emphasizing details or removing distractions.

8. Panorama and HDR Stitching: Learn how to create stunning panoramic images and high dynamic range (HDR) images using post-processing software. Combine multiple shots to create a seamless panorama or merge bracketed exposures to capture a wider dynamic range.

9. Presets and Batch Processing: Discover the convenience of using presets, which are pre-defined settings or adjustments that can be applied to multiple images. Explore how to create your own presets or use pre-made presets to streamline your workflow and maintain a consistent look across your images.

10. Workflow and Organization: Develop an efficient post-processing workflow to manage and organize your images effectively. Learn how to import, cull, and rate your images, as well as keywording and metadata management for easy retrieval.

Post-processing is a creative and subjective process that allows you to put your personal touch on your nature and wildlife photographs. It provides endless possibilities for enhancing the beauty and impact of your images while staying true to your vision and style. Whether you prefer a natural and realistic look or more artistic and creative interpretations, post-processing software and tools are essential companions in your journey to capturing the beauty of nature through your lens.

Techniques for enhancing and optimizing nature and wildlife photographs

Enhancing and optimizing nature and wildlife photographs involves various techniques and considerations to bring out the best in your images. Here are some key techniques to consider:

1. Exposure and Contrast Adjustments: Ensure that your image has proper exposure by adjusting the brightness and contrast. Enhance the overall tonal range by adjusting the shadows and highlights to reveal details in both dark and bright areas.

2. Color Correction: Fine-tune the colors in your photograph to achieve a natural and pleasing look. Adjust the white balance to ensure accurate color representation, and make adjustments to saturation, vibrance, and hue to enhance the colors present in the scene.

3. Sharpening and Detail Enhancement: Apply sharpening techniques to enhance the clarity and details in your image. Use sharpening tools selectively to avoid over-sharpening and introducing artifacts. Additionally, consider using clarity adjustments to enhance mid-tone contrast and bring out texture.

4. Noise Reduction: When photographing wildlife, particularly in low-light conditions, noise can be a challenge. Apply noise reduction techniques to minimize digital noise while preserving important details. Strike a balance between reducing noise and maintaining image sharpness.

5. Cropping and Composition: Consider cropping your image to improve its composition and eliminate distractions. Experiment with different crop ratios and aspect ratios to create a visually pleasing and balanced composition. Remember to maintain sufficient resolution for printing or display purposes.

6. Depth of Field Control: Use selective focus and depth of field to draw attention to your subject. Depending on the scene and your artistic vision, you may choose to have a shallow depth of field to isolate the subject or a larger depth of field to capture more details in the foreground and background.

7. Cloning and Healing: Remove any distracting elements or imperfections in your image using cloning and healing tools. Clean up dust spots, sensor spots, or any unwanted objects that may detract from the overall image quality.

8. Creative Effects: Experiment with creative effects such as vignetting, split toning, or selective color adjustments to add a unique touch to your images. Be mindful of using effects in moderation to maintain a natural and believable look.

9. Graduated Filters and Gradient Masks: Utilize graduated filters or gradient masks to balance exposure in scenes with a significant contrast between the sky and the foreground. Graduated filters can help control the brightness of the sky while maintaining the desired exposure in the rest of the image.

10. Final Image Optimization: Before finalizing your image, check for any remaining imperfections or distractions. Pay attention to small details such as sensor spots, chromatic aberration, or lens distortion, and correct them if necessary. Ensure the final image is properly sharpened and ready for display or printing.

Remember, enhancing and optimizing your nature and wildlife

photographs is a creative process that should be guided by your artistic vision and the story you want to convey. Experiment with different techniques, but always strive to maintain the authenticity and integrity of the scene. With practice and attention to detail, you can bring out the full potential of your nature and wildlife images, capturing the beauty and wonder of the natural world.

Preserving the authenticity of the image while enhancing its visual impact

Preserving the authenticity of a nature or wildlife image while enhancing its visual impact is a delicate balance that requires careful consideration. Here are some tips to help you achieve this:

1. Retain the Essence: Keep in mind the original atmosphere and mood of the scene you captured. Avoid over-editing that may alter the natural feel or misrepresent the subject. Strive to preserve the authenticity and integrity of the moment you captured.

2. Enhance Rather than Transform: Instead of drastically altering the image, focus on enhancing its existing qualities. Enhance the natural colors, details, and textures to bring out the beauty that was already present. Avoid excessive manipulation that may make the image appear unnatural or heavily edited.

3. Use Subtle Adjustments: Make subtle adjustments to the overall tonal range, contrast, and saturation to enhance the visual impact without sacrificing the authenticity. Pay attention to the subtle details and nuances in the image, ensuring that they remain intact and true to the original scene.

4. Maintain Balance: While enhancing certain elements of the image, ensure that the overall balance and harmony are maintained. Avoid emphasizing one aspect at the expense of others, as this may distort the original intent of the photograph.

5. Preserve the Natural Environment: If you are

photographing wildlife in its natural habitat, respect the environment and avoid altering or removing elements that are integral to the scene. Keep in mind the ethical considerations of nature photography and strive to leave minimal impact on the subject and its surroundings.

6. Seek Feedback: Share your work with fellow photographers or trusted mentors to get constructive feedback. They can provide valuable insights and help you gauge if the enhancements you've made align with the authenticity of the image.

Remember, the goal is to enhance the visual impact of the image while staying true to the authenticity and beauty of nature. Each photograph has its own unique story to tell, and by preserving the authenticity, you can create compelling and impactful images that resonate with viewers and evoke a sense of connection to the natural world.

Macro photography: Exploring the intricate details of nature up close

Macro photography allows us to explore the intricate details of nature up close, revealing a hidden world that is often overlooked by the naked eye. It is a fascinating genre that opens up a whole new realm of photographic possibilities.

In macro photography, the primary objective is to capture the fine details and textures of small subjects such as flowers, insects, and other tiny creatures. By getting up close and personal, we can reveal the stunning patterns, textures, and colors that are often unseen in the larger context of the natural world.

To excel in macro photography, it requires a combination of technical skill, patience, and a keen eye for detail. Here are some key aspects to consider when exploring the world of macro photography:

1. Equipment: Invest in a macro lens specifically designed for close-up photography. These lenses have a high magnification ratio and allow you to focus on subjects at very short distances. Additionally, consider using a tripod to ensure stability and sharpness in your images, as macro photography often requires precise focusing.

2. Lighting: Pay attention to lighting as it plays a crucial role in macro photography. Natural light can provide beautiful results, especially during the golden hours when the light is soft and warm. Alternatively, you can experiment with diffused artificial light sources or use reflectors and diffusers to control the intensity and

direction of light.

3. Depth of Field: Due to the close proximity to the subject, achieving a sufficient depth of field can be challenging in macro photography. Consider using a small aperture (high f-number) to increase the depth of field and ensure that your subject is sharp from front to back. However, be mindful of potential diffraction that may occur at extremely small apertures.

4. Composition: Composition is just as important in macro photography as in any other genre. Pay attention to the placement of your subject, the arrangement of elements within the frame, and the use of leading lines, patterns, and textures to create visually appealing compositions.

5. Patience and Observation: Macro photography requires patience and a keen sense of observation. Take the time to study your subjects, their behaviors, and the details you want to capture. Be prepared to spend time waiting for the perfect moment or exploring different angles to capture the subject from its most captivating perspective.

6. Post-processing: Post-processing can play a role in enhancing the details, colors, and overall impact of your macro photographs. However, strive to maintain the natural look and feel of the subject while enhancing its inherent beauty. Use post-processing techniques such as selective sharpening, contrast adjustments, and color correction to bring out the best in your macro images.

Macro photography offers a unique opportunity to delve into the world of small-scale wonders and explore the intricacies of nature up close. By mastering the technical aspects and employing your artistic vision, you can capture stunning images that showcase the beauty and marvels of the tiny world that surrounds us.

Bird and wildlife photography: Techniques for capturing fast-moving subjects

Bird and wildlife photography is a thrilling and challenging genre that requires specialized techniques to capture fast-moving subjects in their natural habitats. To successfully photograph birds and wildlife, it is essential to understand their behavior, use the right equipment, and employ specific techniques to freeze the action and capture compelling images. Here are some key techniques to consider:

1. Equipment: Invest in a telephoto lens with a long focal length to bring distant subjects closer and capture fine details. A lens with a fast autofocus system and image stabilization can be advantageous for tracking and capturing fast-moving subjects. Additionally, consider using a sturdy tripod or a monopod for added stability.

2. Research and Observation: Study the behavior and habitats of the birds and wildlife you wish to photograph. Knowing their habits and preferred locations will increase your chances of getting close to them and capturing unique moments. Patience and keen observation are crucial for anticipating their movements and behaviors.

3. Fast Shutter Speeds: Use a fast shutter speed to freeze the motion and capture sharp images of fast-moving subjects. A minimum shutter speed of 1/1000th of a second is often recommended, but you may need even faster speeds depending on the subject and its speed of movement.

4. Continuous Shooting Mode: Switch your camera to continuous shooting mode to capture a rapid sequence of frames. This allows you to increase the chances of getting a perfectly timed shot and a series of images that depict the subject's movement.

5. Autofocus and Tracking: Utilize the autofocus and tracking capabilities of your camera to keep your subject in focus. Use the appropriate autofocus mode, such as continuous autofocus (AI Servo for Canon or AF-C for Nikon), to track and maintain focus on the moving subject. Experiment with different autofocus points and area modes to find what works best for your shooting situation.

6. Composition and Background: Pay attention to composition and background to create visually appealing images. Use the rule of thirds, leading lines, and negative space to enhance the visual impact of your photographs. Additionally, choose backgrounds that complement and highlight your subject, avoiding distracting elements that may take away from the main focus.

7. Patience and Fieldcraft: Wildlife photography requires patience and fieldcraft skills. Learn to blend into the environment, move slowly and quietly, and minimize disturbances to the subjects. By being patient and observant, you increase your chances of capturing natural behaviors and intimate moments.

8. Ethics and Conservation: Always prioritize the well-being and safety of the animals. Follow ethical guidelines for wildlife photography, respect their habitats, and avoid causing stress or harm to the subjects. Be mindful of local regulations and conservation efforts, and promote responsible wildlife photography.

Bird and wildlife photography can be a thrilling and rewarding experience, allowing you to document the beauty and diversity of the natural world. With the right equipment, knowledge, and techniques, you can capture stunning images that showcase the majesty and fascinating behaviors of birds and wildlife.

Landscape photography: Creating breathtaking vistas and capturing natural wonders

Landscape photography is a captivating genre that allows you to capture the beauty and grandeur of the natural world. Whether you're photographing sweeping vistas, serene seascapes, majestic mountains, or tranquil forests, the goal is to create images that evoke a sense of awe and convey the essence of the landscape. Here are some techniques to help you create breathtaking landscape photographs:

1. Composition: Composition plays a vital role in landscape photography. Use the rule of thirds, leading lines, and foreground interest to create a visually pleasing and balanced composition. Experiment with different perspectives and angles to add depth and dimension to your images.

2. Golden Hour: Take advantage of the magical light during the golden hour, which occurs around sunrise and sunset. The soft, warm light during this time adds a beautiful glow to the landscape, enhances colors, and creates long, dramatic shadows. Plan your shoots accordingly to make the most of this enchanting light.

3. Wide-Angle Lens: Use a wide-angle lens to capture the vastness of the landscape and include a broad field of view. Wide-angle lenses can help you emphasize the foreground and create a sense of depth in your images. Experiment with different focal lengths to find the best

lens for each scene.

4. Aperture and Depth of Field: Adjust your aperture to control the depth of field in your landscape photographs. A smaller aperture (higher f-number) such as f/11 or f/16 will result in a larger depth of field, keeping both the foreground and background in focus. However, don't be afraid to experiment with shallow depth of field for creative effects, such as focusing on a specific subject or creating a dreamy background.

5. Tripod and Stability: Use a sturdy tripod to keep your camera steady, especially when shooting in low light conditions or using longer exposures. This ensures sharpness and allows you to capture fine details in the landscape. Additionally, use a remote shutter release or the camera's built-in self-timer to minimize camera shake.

6. Filters: Consider using filters to enhance your landscape photographs. Graduated neutral density (ND) filters can help balance the exposure between the sky and the land, while polarizing filters can reduce glare and enhance colors, particularly in water and foliage. Experiment with different filters to achieve the desired effects.

7. Weather and Atmosphere: Pay attention to weather conditions and how they can impact the mood and atmosphere of your landscape photographs. Stormy skies, dramatic clouds, mist, and fog can add a sense of drama and mystery to your images. Be patient and flexible, as weather conditions can change quickly and offer unique opportunities.

8. Post-Processing: Post-processing is an integral part of landscape photography. Use software like Adobe Lightroom or Photoshop to enhance colors, adjust tones, and fine-tune your images. However, strive to maintain a natural and realistic look while enhancing the inherent beauty of the landscape.

Remember, landscape photography is not just about capturing the physical aspects of the scenery but also conveying the emotions and sense of wonder that the landscape evokes. Embrace the beauty of nature, immerse yourself in the surroundings, and let your creativity guide you in capturing breathtaking vistas and natural wonders.

The role of nature photographers as advocates for conservation

Nature photographers play a crucial role as advocates for conservation through their powerful images. By capturing and sharing the beauty and vulnerability of the natural world, they raise awareness about environmental issues and inspire people to take action to protect and preserve our planet. Here are some ways in which nature photographers contribute to conservation:

1. Creating Emotional Connections: Nature photographers have the ability to evoke strong emotions through their images. They can capture the majesty of endangered species, the fragility of ecosystems, and the impact of human activities on the environment. By sharing these images, they help people develop a deep emotional connection to nature, fostering a sense of empathy and responsibility towards the natural world.

2. Education and Awareness: Nature photographers are educators at heart. Through their photographs, they provide valuable information about ecosystems, species, and environmental challenges. They can shed light on lesser-known issues and highlight the importance of conservation efforts. Their images can be used in publications, exhibitions, and educational materials to raise awareness and educate people about the need to protect biodiversity.

3. Conservation Partnerships: Many nature photographers actively collaborate with conservation organizations and scientists to support their work. They contribute

their images for research, campaigns, and fundraising efforts. By working closely with conservation groups, they can amplify the impact of their photographs and contribute directly to conservation initiatives.

4. Influencing Public Opinion: Nature photographers have the power to shape public opinion and influence attitudes towards conservation. Through their captivating images, they can challenge misconceptions, debunk myths, and inspire positive change. Their photographs can reach a wide audience through exhibitions, publications, online platforms, and social media, creating a ripple effect that can lead to increased support for conservation efforts.

5. Conservation Stories: Nature photographers often tell compelling stories through their images, highlighting the interconnectedness of species and ecosystems. They can document success stories of conservation projects, showcasing the positive outcomes of conservation efforts. By sharing these stories, they motivate and inspire others to get involved in conservation activities and make a difference.

6. Advocacy and Policy: Nature photographers can use their platform to advocate for stronger environmental policies and regulations. They can raise their voices and use their images to shed light on environmental issues that require urgent attention. Their photographs can be instrumental in influencing decision-makers, policymakers, and the public to prioritize conservation and take steps towards sustainable practices.

Nature photographers have the unique ability to capture the beauty, diversity, and fragility of the natural world. Through their images, they become storytellers, educators, and advocates for conservation. By using their skills and passion, they contribute to the global effort to protect and preserve our planet for future generations.

Promoting ethical practices and minimizing the impact on wildlife and habitats

Promoting ethical practices and minimizing the impact on wildlife and habitats is of utmost importance for nature photographers. Here are some guidelines and principles that nature photographers should follow:

1. Respect Wildlife and Habitats: Photographers should prioritize the welfare and safety of wildlife and their habitats. It is essential to observe animals from a safe distance and avoid disturbing their natural behavior. Photographers should never bait, trap, or handle wildlife for the sake of a photograph.

2. Know and Follow Local Regulations: It is crucial to be aware of and adhere to local laws and regulations regarding wildlife protection and conservation. These regulations may include restrictions on approaching certain species, entering protected areas, or using certain photography techniques. Respecting these regulations ensures the well-being of wildlife and helps preserve their habitats.

3. Practice Minimal Impact Techniques: Photographers should strive to minimize their impact on the environment and wildlife. This includes staying on designated trails or paths, using non-intrusive camera gear and techniques, and avoiding any actions that may damage or disturb the natural surroundings. Leave no trace and leave the habitat as you found it.

4. Be Patient and Observant: Patience is key in wildlife

photography. Rather than chasing after animals, photographers should take the time to observe their behavior and movements. By understanding the natural patterns and habitats of the subjects, photographers can capture more authentic and undisturbed moments.

5. Educate and Inform: Nature photographers have a unique opportunity to educate their audience about the importance of ethical practices. Through their images and accompanying captions or articles, they can share information about wildlife conservation, the need for habitat preservation, and responsible photography practices. This helps create awareness and encourages others to adopt ethical approaches when photographing nature.

6. Support Conservation Efforts: Nature photographers can contribute to conservation by supporting local conservation organizations and initiatives. This can be through donations, volunteering, or actively participating in citizen science programs. By giving back to the environments and wildlife they photograph, photographers can contribute to long-term conservation efforts.

By embracing ethical practices and minimizing their impact on wildlife and habitats, nature photographers can not only capture stunning images but also contribute to the preservation of the natural world. It is the responsibility of every nature photographer to prioritize the well-being of the subjects they photograph and to promote conservation values through their work.

The power of photography in raising awareness and inspiring action

Photography has a powerful impact in raising awareness and inspiring action, especially when it comes to nature and wildlife conservation. Here's how photography can make a difference:

1. Eliciting Emotional Connections: Captivating nature and wildlife photographs have the ability to evoke strong emotions in viewers. When people connect emotionally with a photograph, they are more likely to care about the subject and feel compelled to take action.

2. Creating Visual Narratives: Photographs tell stories, and through visual narratives, photographers can highlight the beauty, fragility, and importance of nature and wildlife. By capturing compelling moments and showcasing the wonders of the natural world, photographers can inspire viewers to appreciate and protect our planet.

3. Fostering Empathy and Understanding: Nature photography has the power to bridge the gap between humans and the natural world. By showcasing the diversity and interconnectedness of ecosystems, photographers can foster empathy and understanding, helping people realize the intrinsic value of preserving our environment.

4. Advocacy and Conservation Campaigns: Photographs often become powerful tools in advocacy and conservation campaigns. They can be used in publications, exhibitions, social media, and other

platforms to shed light on environmental issues, raise awareness about endangered species, and promote sustainable practices. Visual storytelling through photography can reach a wide audience and motivate individuals, communities, and governments to take action.

5. Education and Communication: Photographs can serve as educational tools, helping people learn about different species, habitats, and environmental challenges. They can also communicate complex scientific concepts in a visually engaging manner, making it easier for people to grasp and remember important information.

6. Inspiring Personal Change: A single photograph has the potential to change someone's perspective and inspire personal change. Whether it's adopting more sustainable lifestyle choices, supporting conservation organizations, or getting involved in local environmental initiatives, photography can motivate individuals to make a positive difference in their own lives and communities.

Through their lens, nature and wildlife photographers have the ability to ignite passion, spark curiosity, and instigate action. By capturing the beauty and fragility of the natural world, they can raise awareness, inspire empathy, and drive positive change. Photography has the power to connect us with the wonders of nature, reminding us of our shared responsibility to protect and preserve it for future generations.

Building a portfolio of nature and wildlife photographs

Building a portfolio of nature and wildlife photographs is an exciting journey that requires time, dedication, and a keen eye for capturing the beauty of the natural world. Here are some tips to help you create a compelling portfolio:

1. Define Your Focus: Determine the specific niche or theme within nature and wildlife photography that you want to showcase in your portfolio. It could be landscapes, birds, mammals, underwater, or any other specific area of interest. Having a focused portfolio will demonstrate your expertise and help you stand out.

2. Curate Your Best Work: Select your strongest and most impactful images that showcase your technical skills, creativity, and unique perspective. Quality over quantity is key. Aim for a cohesive collection that tells a story or highlights a particular aspect of nature.

3. Show Diversity: While having a niche is important, it's also essential to demonstrate versatility in your portfolio. Include a variety of subjects, compositions, lighting conditions, and locations. This diversity will showcase your range as a photographer and capture the breadth of the natural world.

4. Emphasize Composition and Technical Excellence: Pay attention to the composition of your photographs. Use the rule of thirds, leading lines, and other composition techniques to create visually pleasing images. Ensure that your images are sharp, properly exposed, and well-

processed to showcase your technical skills.

5. Tell a Story: Aim to create a narrative within your portfolio. Organize your images in a way that flows and tells a story about the natural world. Show the behavior of animals, the interaction between species, or the changing seasons to evoke a sense of connection and emotion.

6. Continuously Improve: A portfolio is a representation of your current skill level, but it should also reflect your growth as a photographer. Keep challenging yourself, experimenting with new techniques, and seeking opportunities to refine your craft. Regularly update your portfolio with your best and latest work.

7. Seek Feedback: Share your portfolio with fellow photographers, mentors, or online photography communities to receive constructive feedback. It can help you gain valuable insights, identify areas for improvement, and refine your portfolio.

8. Presentation Matters: Consider the presentation format for your portfolio. Create a visually appealing and user-friendly online portfolio or consider printing your images for a physical portfolio. Pay attention to the layout, organization, and overall aesthetics to ensure a professional and impactful presentation.

Remember, building a strong portfolio takes time and continuous effort. As you grow as a photographer, your portfolio should evolve and reflect your unique style and vision. Be patient, persevere, and let your passion for nature and wildlife shine through your images.

Opportunities for exhibiting and publishing your work

Exhibiting and publishing your nature and wildlife photographs can provide valuable exposure, recognition, and opportunities to reach a wider audience. Here are some avenues to consider:

1. Nature and Wildlife Photography Contests: Participate in local, national, and international photography contests specifically focused on nature and wildlife. Winning or being shortlisted in these competitions can give your work significant visibility and credibility.

2. Art Galleries and Exhibitions: Approach art galleries, museums, nature centers, or other exhibition spaces that showcase photography. Pitch your portfolio and inquire about potential exhibition opportunities. Solo or group exhibitions can expose your work to art enthusiasts, collectors, and the general public.

3. Photography Festivals and Events: Look for photography festivals, workshops, and conferences that feature nature and wildlife photography. These events often include exhibitions or portfolio reviews, providing opportunities to connect with industry professionals, fellow photographers, and potential buyers.

4. Nature and Wildlife Magazines: Submit your work to magazines specializing in nature, wildlife, and outdoor photography. Many publications have dedicated sections or features where they showcase selected photographs from talented photographers. Getting published in these magazines can offer exposure and

recognition within the photography community.

5. Online Platforms and Photography Websites: Utilize online platforms and photography websites to showcase your work. Create a portfolio website or join photography communities that allow you to display and share your photographs. Online platforms also provide opportunities to sell prints or license your images.

6. Stock Photography Agencies: Consider submitting your nature and wildlife photographs to stock photography agencies. These agencies offer a platform for licensing your images to be used in various commercial applications such as advertisements, websites, and publications.

7. Collaborations and Exhibitions with Conservation Organizations: Connect with local or global conservation organizations that align with your values and interests. Collaborate on projects, exhibitions, or publications that promote the beauty and importance of nature and wildlife while raising awareness about conservation efforts.

8. Self-Publishing: Explore self-publishing options to create your own photo book or e-book featuring your nature and wildlife photographs. This allows you to have complete control over the content and presentation of your work, and you can market and sell it independently.

Remember to research and tailor your submissions to specific opportunities, follow submission guidelines, and present your work professionally. Networking, building relationships within the industry, and leveraging social media can also help you discover new opportunities and connect with like-minded individuals.

Sharing your passion for nature photography through digital platforms and social media

In today's digital age, sharing your passion for nature photography through online platforms and social media can have a significant impact in reaching and engaging with a wide audience. Here are some tips for effectively sharing your work:

1. Create a Photography Blog or Website: Establish a dedicated blog or website where you can showcase your nature photographs, share stories, and provide insights into your creative process. This platform serves as a centralized hub for your work and allows you to build an online portfolio.

2. Engage on Social Media: Utilize social media platforms such as Instagram, Facebook, Twitter, and YouTube to share your nature photographs. Regularly post your best work, share behind-the-scenes stories, and engage with your audience through comments and messages. Use relevant hashtags to reach a larger audience and connect with other photographers and nature enthusiasts.

3. Tell Compelling Stories: Share the stories behind your photographs. Explain the inspiration, the location, and any interesting encounters or experiences you had while capturing the image. Use captions or blog posts to provide context and engage your audience on a deeper level.

4. Participate in Photography Communities: Join online photography communities and forums where you can share your work, receive feedback, and connect

with fellow photographers. Engage in constructive discussions, participate in themed photo challenges, and learn from others in the community.

5. Collaborate with Influencers and Brands: Explore collaboration opportunities with influencers, brands, and organizations that align with your values and target audience. Collaborative projects can help expand your reach and expose your work to new audiences.

6. Offer Photography Tips and Tutorials: Share your knowledge and expertise by offering photography tips, tutorials, and behind-the-scenes insights. This not only positions you as an authority in the field but also provides value to your audience and encourages them to engage with your content.

7. Engage with Your Audience: Respond to comments, messages, and inquiries from your audience. Engaging with your followers builds a sense of community and encourages them to continue supporting and sharing your work.

8. Cross-Promote with Like-Minded Individuals: Collaborate with other nature photographers, outdoor enthusiasts, or relevant influencers to cross-promote each other's work. This allows you to tap into their audience while providing exposure to their followers as well.

Remember to maintain a consistent and visually appealing online presence, adhere to copyright and licensing guidelines when sharing your work, and always give credit to other photographers or artists when appropriate. By leveraging digital platforms and social media, you can effectively share your passion for nature photography and inspire others to appreciate the beauty of the natural world.

Interviews and profiles of renowned nature and wildlife photographers

1. Interview with Ansel Adams: Exploring the Legacy of Black and White Landscape Photography
   - Insights into Adams' iconic landscape photography style and his dedication to environmental conservation.
2. Profile: Frans Lanting - Master of Wildlife Photography
   - Delving into Lanting's remarkable career and his ability to capture intimate moments in the animal kingdom.
3. Interview with Cristina Mittermeier: Conservation through Photography
   - Discussing Mittermeier's work as a conservation photographer and her efforts to raise awareness about marine ecosystems.
4. Profile: Art Wolfe - Celebrating the Diversity of Nature
   - Examining Wolfe's extensive portfolio and his talent for capturing the unique beauty of wildlife and landscapes around the world.
5. Interview with Steve McCurry: Portraits of the Human Connection to Nature
   - Unveiling McCurry's storytelling approach and his ability to capture the human-nature relationship through his lens.
6. Profile: Michael "Nick" Nichols - Pioneering Wildlife Photojournalism
   - Exploring Nichols' groundbreaking work for

National Geographic and his contributions to wildlife photojournalism.

7. Interview with Ami Vitale: Documenting Conservation Stories through Photography
   - Delving into Vitale's experiences documenting the efforts of communities and organizations in wildlife conservation.

8. Profile: Thomas Mangelsen - Capturing the Majesty of Wildlife
   - Celebrating Mangelsen's lifelong commitment to photographing endangered species and his passion for wildlife preservation.

These interviews and profiles offer insights into the lives and works of renowned nature and wildlife photographers, showcasing their unique perspectives, approaches, and contributions to the field.

Their experiences, challenges, and insights into capturing the beauty of nature

1. Overcoming the Elements: Photographing in Extreme Environments
   - Exploring how photographers tackle challenges such as harsh weather conditions, remote locations, and unpredictable wildlife encounters.
2. Patience and Perseverance: The Art of Waiting for the Perfect Shot
   - Sharing stories of photographers spending hours or even days waiting for the ideal moment to capture a rare or elusive wildlife sighting.
3. Connecting with Nature: Finding Inspiration in the Outdoors
   - Reflecting on how spending time in nature and developing a deep appreciation for the environment can influence a photographer's creative process.
4. Conservation and Education: Using Photography to Raise Awareness
   - Shedding light on how photographers advocate for environmental causes and use their images to educate the public about conservation issues.
5. Ethics and Responsibility: Respecting Wildlife and Their Habitats

- Discussing the importance of ethical practices in wildlife photography, including maintaining a safe distance, minimizing disturbance, and respecting animal behavior.

6. Behind the Lens: The Emotional and Spiritual Impact of Nature Photography
   - Exploring the transformative power of nature photography on the photographers themselves, including moments of awe, connection, and introspection.

7. The Art of Composition: Balancing Aesthetics and Authenticity
   - Examining the creative decisions photographers make in composing their images to evoke a sense of beauty, harmony, and storytelling.

8. Tools of the Trade: Cameras, Lenses, and Equipment for Nature Photography
   - Offering insights into the gear and equipment preferred by experienced nature photographers and how they optimize their tools for capturing the natural world.

These experiences, challenges, and insights shared by nature photographers provide a deeper understanding of the dedication, passion, and technical skill required to capture the breathtaking beauty of the natural world.

Learning from their techniques and perspectives

1. Mastering Light: Understanding how photographers manipulate natural light to create stunning and evocative images.
2. Composing with Purpose: Exploring different composition techniques and how they can enhance the visual impact of nature photographs.
3. Patience and Observation: Learning how to observe and anticipate animal behavior to capture captivating moments in the wild.
4. Finding Unique Perspectives: Discovering innovative ways to capture familiar subjects and landscapes, offering fresh and compelling perspectives.
5. Post-Processing for Impact: Understanding the role of post-processing techniques in enhancing and refining nature photographs while maintaining their authenticity.
6. Telling a Story: Learning how to weave a narrative through a series of photographs, capturing the essence and spirit of a place or species.
7. Technical Mastery: Acquiring advanced technical skills, such as using specialized equipment, long-exposure techniques, and focus stacking, to achieve professional-quality nature photographs.
8. Ethical Considerations: Understanding and adhering to ethical guidelines in wildlife photography, respecting the well-being of animals and their habitats.
9. Connecting with the Natural World: Exploring the profound connection between photographers and nature, and how it can enhance creativity and

photographic expression.

10. Inspiring Conservation: Discovering how photographers use their images to raise awareness, inspire action, and contribute to conservation efforts.

By studying the techniques and perspectives of renowned nature photographers, readers can gain valuable insights and inspiration to elevate their own nature photography skills and create impactful images that celebrate the beauty and importance of the natural world.

Reflecting on the impact of nature and wildlife photography

Nature and wildlife photography has a profound impact on individuals and society as a whole. Through the lens, photographers have the power to evoke emotions, raise awareness, and inspire action. The captivating images of breathtaking landscapes, intricate details of flora and fauna, and intimate moments in the animal kingdom provide a glimpse into the beauty and fragility of our natural world.

Nature and wildlife photographs have the ability to awaken a sense of wonder and awe, reminding us of the incredible diversity and interconnectedness of life on Earth. They have the power to ignite curiosity, instill a sense of responsibility, and deepen our connection to nature. These images transport us to remote corners of the world, exposing us to the wonders of the natural environment that we may never have the opportunity to experience firsthand.

Furthermore, nature and wildlife photography serves as a powerful tool for conservation. It captures the essence of threatened ecosystems and endangered species, highlighting the urgent need for their protection. By showcasing the vulnerability and beauty of our natural world, photographers play a vital role in advocating for environmental conservation and sustainability.

The impact of nature and wildlife photography extends beyond aesthetic appreciation. It has the potential to shift perspectives, change behaviors, and drive positive change. These photographs can inspire individuals to take action, whether it be through supporting conservation initiatives, making sustainable choices, or actively engaging in environmental advocacy.

"Through the Lens: Capturing the Beauty of Nature and Wildlife" invites readers to embark on a visual journey, celebrating the power of nature and wildlife photography to transform our perceptions and ignite a sense of responsibility towards the natural world. It encourages us to pause, appreciate, and protect the beauty and biodiversity that surrounds us, reminding us of the interconnectedness of all life and the importance of preserving our planet for future generations.

Encouragement to continue exploring and appreciating the beauty of the natural world "Through the Lens"

As you delve into the captivating pages of "Through the Lens: Capturing the Beauty of Nature and Wildlife," I invite you to embark on a personal journey of exploration and appreciation. Open your eyes to the intricate details of a delicate flower, the majestic grandeur of a mountain range, and the fleeting moments of wildlife in their natural habitat. Let the images transport you to breathtaking landscapes and evoke a sense of wonder and awe.

Take a moment to reconnect with the beauty of the natural world and allow yourself to be captivated by its boundless diversity. Through the lens, you have the opportunity to witness the extraordinary and discover the hidden gems that lie in every corner of our planet. Engage your senses and immerse yourself in the sights, sounds, and emotions captured within each photograph.

As you turn the pages, let the photographs inspire you to explore and experience nature firsthand. Venture into the great outdoors, whether it be a nearby park, a distant wilderness, or even your own backyard. Observe the intricate ecosystems, observe the vibrant colors, and feel the rhythm of life that surrounds you.

Remember that you too can become a storyteller through the lens. Capture the beauty and moments that resonate with you, and share them with the world. Your photographs have the power to inspire, educate, and spark a deeper connection to nature.

Embrace the challenges and rewards of photographing the natural world, and let your passion guide you on a never-ending journey of discovery.

May "Through the Lens: Capturing the Beauty of Nature and Wildlife" serve as a constant source of inspiration, reminding you to appreciate and protect the wonders of the natural world. With each photograph, let us continue to celebrate the beauty, diversity, and fragility of our planet, nurturing a deep sense of stewardship and ensuring a sustainable future for generations to come.